MW01108005

In these new poems Herbert Woodward Martin once again shows his virtuosity as a poet with a wonderfully tuned ear and a command of the rhythmical line. In poem after poem, I found myself "flowing along," sometimes with an Alabama cotton tenant farmer's wife, sometimes with an old woman peeling an apple (for he is definitely a shape-shifter in many of these poems), but usually with the assured, declarative voice of a speaker who has reached the peak of his powers.

But there is more: these poems also demonstrate a need not only to go beyond the self, but also to contest the limits of poetry itself. Prose poems such as "Black Prometheus" and "American Gothic," and lone-lined poems such as "Hurrying" and "To Bedlam and Back" are as rhythmical and musical as lined verse, but they present such a density of details and thoughts it's as though each poem contained its own small world, a world the reader finds himself immersed in, and relishing.

The poems throughout *Escape to the Promised Land* show the spirit of the poet at work with his losses and loves, and the result is a book of deeply human and poetical power.

—Len Roberts

Other Books by Herbert Woodward Martin

New York, The Nine Million and Other Poems (Abracadabra
        Press)
The Shit-Storm Poems (Pilot Press)
The Persistence of The Flesh (Lotus Press)
The Forms of Silence (Lotus Press)
Galileo's Sun in *Suns and Dominions* (Bottom Dog Press)
The Log of The Vigilante (Mellen Poetry Press)

He co-edited *In His Own Voice: The Dramatic and Other Uncollected
        Works of Paul Laurence Dunbar* (Ohio University Press)
Paul Laurence Dunbar: Selected Poems (Penguin Press)

About:
*Herbert Woodward Martin and The African American Tradition in
        Poetry* (Kent State University Press)

Escape To the Promised Land

Herbert Woodward Martin

Paul Laurence Dunbar Series
Bottom Dog Press
Huron, OH

© 2005

Herbert Woodward Martin/ Bottom Dog Press Inc.

ISBN 0-933087-92-6

Bottom Dog Press

PO Box 425/ Huron, OH 44839

Lsmithdog@aol.com

http://members.aol.com/Lsmithdog/bottomdog

Cover art "The Migration of the Negro" Panel 3

by Jacob Lawrence

Acknowledgments

"Advent" *Windhover;* "The Washer Woman's Fire"*Grand Street;* "Approaching The New Year"*Chaminade Review;* "Architecture" *The Heartlands;* "A Childhood Memory"*Aura Literary / Arts;* "Congregational Windows" *Kerf;* "Fragment for Emily Dickinson" *Iota;* "Breath" *Kerf;* "Appropriate Words for Mourning"*Stand;* "Walker Evans' "Alabama Cotton. . ." *10 Michigan Poets—An Anthology;* "Walker Evans' "Alabama Tenant. . . 1936" *Midwest Poetry Review;* "The Garden of Earthly Delight" *Writers' Forum;* "Turning Around" *West Wind;* "Shadow of Light" *Manifold;* "Neighbor" *George Washington Review;* "Shalom, Chaver" *Pulsar;* "Hustling" *Confluence;* "Csontvary Tivadar's "Old Woman . . ." *Nexus;* "There Once Was an Old Woman" *Mavrick;* "Playing Until Forgetfulness Comes" *The Massachusetts Review;* "Dark Pronouncement" *Oxford Magazine;* "Elvis Presley's First Appearance. . ." *All Shook Up: An Anthology, The University of Arkansas Press;* "The Season of War" *Nexus;* "Here" *Jeopardy;* "Sleeping Lovers" *Cottonwood;* "Painful Laughter" *Manifold;* "Where The Wild Nettles Grow" *House Organ;* "Lawd Chile" Originally titled "At The Five and Dime" *Broadside Press;* "American Tourist"*Out of Line.*

My deepest thanks to The Ohio Arts Council and to The Montgomery Arts and Cultural Districts for the two fellowships which allowed me to complete this manuscript.

Paul Laurence Dunbar Series General Editor: David Shevin

Ohio Arts Council
A STATE AGENCY
THAT SUPPORTS PUBLIC
PROGRAMS IN THE ARTS

Contents

This volume is dedicated to the sacred memory
of two poets and two colleagues without whose affection
I might never have survived.

Raymond R. Patterson (1929-2001)
Calvin C. Hernton (1934-2001)
Joseph S. McNamara (1940 -2002)
John M. McCaffery (1938 -2003)

This volume is also inscribed with love for
my daughter and granddaughters:

Julia Johanna Martin
Marina Sheree Worley
Christian Taylor Lovett
Athena Rose Croker

I. Hungry Dilemmas of Word and Spirits

ADVENT

There is something
tedious about
babysitting
unless you can
teach the baby
table-tennis
and show him or her
the magic
of a rebounding
pong that possesses
a spirit descending
like twilight
like Christ coming
for a second time.

THE TONGUES OF OLD MEN

The company of night
Prowls the delicate air.
In the region of the soul
The poverty of dreams face
Certain hungry dilemmas of
Words and spirits to bare
An answer taken from the
Tongues of old men who
Resided in the country
Of death, in the delicate
Silence where they came
Face to face with the
Night of dying memory.

THE WASHER WOMAN'S FIRE

My immigrant mother cooked her white clothes alive
From dawn to five she boiled them, turned them over,
Then she removed them and said: "You must whip the dirt
From your clothes if you want them to be clean."
Then she rinsed them twice and hung them facing Southtown.
There were sheets and pillowcases, ruffles, ties and silks and
    laces.
Every Monday morning my father built her iron pot a fire,
Then filled it with water. Carrying water is a tall command for a
    small
Daughter. The fire seemed always there, so did the pot. On my natal
    day
June 6, 1845, a spark reached beyond that pot and caught a
    ride
On a derelict piece of paper. It was a hungry wind which carried
That torch like a human passion. It stirred the entire community.
It left a trail as it began to eat the dry grasses, then the wood
Frames which shaped the houses; soon Southtown was all aflame.
The fire was quick, abidingly quick. It grew to full life in an hour.
From Diamond to Wood to Water Street smoke and wind were the
    fears
You most likely would meet. The losses were certain; the deaths
    were
Finally tallied and assured. A lunching wind, an enormous fire ball
Swirled around a fireman and burned him through to the blood.
A delicate old woman who refused to leave her home knelt down in
A private place, and all that was left were a gathering of bones
Fused together. When evening came the fire settled gently;
The cinders smoldered. Now when I have cause to remember that
Special day I think of what a sudden, sudden ordering that fire
    made
Of Southtown celebrating my seventh birthday.

APPROACHING THE NEW YEAR IN PECS

For: Laszki Komlosi

The city children bleed an old woman's torment with sweet horns;
They herald the New Year. The old woman sifts through throw
     aways
That no longer merit love. Cherry bombs curse her skin with
Celebration; a rash, a sudden scream textures her body. There
Are no finds, no wastes of bread, no wines left to be drunk.
She looks with devastating concentration; her eyes flash old
Disturbances. She pleads with her innocent tormentors. Her
Complaints are filled with pleasure; the young boys do not
Listen; the young girls convulse with laughter. The adults
Pursue their own ways; women greet the death of the old year; men
Begin to mourn the new in their *palacksor*. They greet and kiss
Old friends naturally. One woman with a voluptuous heart loves
Every male citizen. They bless her with bountiful kisses. Her
Elder is driven by the lust of necessity. She braces herself
Against the particular cold; she moves carefully in her dread
Coat, felt hat and attached purse. She is the lady exquisite in
Public. Her principal days are gone. Fury is her excuse for
Robbing the local trash cans. The sound of anticipation is an
Ache in her spine; her ears are infected with old reminders,
Remote dignities of another time. An attentive father stands
Between the old woman and her hunger. She is unsettled motion.
The air does not spell out her anger clearly. Her fading esteem
Haunts the father; she is too far gone, he can not rescue her
From madness. He watches her conversing with the violet wind
     and
Knows there are no more days of ease for her.

FRIEZE

A
Rose
Lurks like
An elegant
Truth hiding
In the stillness
Of landscape.
It begs for
A draughtsman
Whose compassionate
Skills can trace
A frieze, or <u>bas relief</u>
On the stone
Dark breath of
Our human terror.

——————————— ❧

II. A Hen Dips Snuff

TURNING AROUND

My neighbor's wife loves birds.
This one, apparently looking for death,
Flew inexorably into her viewing window
And broke its neck. It has lain in
The weekend leaves, a wreck of flesh
And mottled feathers. My neighbor
Discovers the body. Knowing his wife's
Love for birds, I say:
"Let's leave it in this pile of leaves
For the collectors. They come on Mondays."
Perhaps, I am not my humane self,
Her husband collaborates, and we hide it
Beneath the leaves, denying it its final
Private place. It is not in me this time
To praise bird or self or light or earth.
I am only able to rake leaves.
They are a distraction to be gathered
Like flakes of snow, or some other dull
Duty which will cause me to turn around.

SENTENCE

I speak for a time
when subtle truths can no longer
withstand the harsh light
of public speech where
the whispers of neighbors
are like pistols of persuasion
firing bullets of anguish
repeatedly aimed at
the shapes of our coming and going.

LAWD CHILE

I done told you a million times
Them words you is fooling around with don't make no sense.
Them words is the devil's work.
You better leave them alone! You hear?
Here you sit from morning to night,
Writing down what you think is right.
Who ever told you,
You had a right to decide bad and good?
It ain't worth the time of day,
Less it's going to bring you some silver,
And I don't see how it's possible for anybody
To be paying you for something
You done scribbled down like chicken scratch.
And don't go tell me nothing 'bout
What or how much money white people make.
You ain't white!
And I don't want to hear nothing 'bout no fame.
Attention ain't no good when you're dead.
Don't make no sense,
And further more, it don't make no never mind,
How much you scream, or how long and wooly
You let your hair grow, or how many baths you refuse to take.
If you ain't got no money, you ain't got nothing to say.
And I didn't have to go to no fool college to learn that.
I done been walking through this world and learning
Since I knowed exactly who I was.
So If I tell you a hen dips snuff,
Search for the box.
Boy where is you going?
I'm talking to you!
You better come back here and listen!
Lawd, Lawd these children are going to be the death of us all
Not that we ain't given them plenty of kindling wood.

PLAYING UNTIL FORGETFULNESS COMES

For: James and Barbara Farrelly

"Remember all the things I have said," then mama went to work.
Summer Mondays are timeless in the hands of boys. The older fam-
ily men harbored nothing but tedium and black failure moving in
their veins. Who in society had ever permitted them to feel one event-
ful day? I know the answer for the men in my family; I watched
each of them die of ignorant neglect. I can not tell you how many
times I watched a soft liquor thirst takes over one of their bodies
and ravage its spirit of decency on that first Monday of the month
when the "Sick and Accident" had to be paid. The insurance money
was always hung in its envelope behind the photography of Jesus.
So we knew where to go when the insurance man said "Collect."
One of those troubled Mondays Uncle Ad reached behind salvation
and removed that protective policy. They took that reserved money
to the local beer garden and traded health and caution for Jack
Daniels. It is still astonishing to me how that money could have
disappeared from behind the family savior without my knowledge.
There are always slights of hand that no one can perceive. When
mama came home from work and discovered that money gone, she
screamed so loud a chill went through the bones of that house. "You
were not mindful of what I said. You were playing instead. Some-
body, somebody was in this house. No kids are suppose to be in
this house when I am at work. How many times do I have to tell
you? So who did you have in here playing? Don't lie to me today;
I'm too tired! Do you know how many hours it took me to earn that
much money just to stay a step ahead of that old insurance man?
That was all the extra money I had this month. He's always at the
door when I ain't got no money, and the one time I'm prepared to
meet him face to face, you go and let some sorry-assed kid in the
house who steals me blind. Go on, get out of my sight before I beat
you both to death." Well, when she was calm and finished crying,
our next door neighbor, who kept her eyes on everything which
happened in the neighborhood said: "Helen those kids didn't do
nothing wrong. They did just what you told them to. It was the
men. I seen them quietly leave out the back way while the kids were
in the front playing and soon they came back with a brown bag
under your uncle's arm, and just before the insurance man came

they left again by the back door staggering like Cooter Brown. Well, I know drunk when I sees it, and that was drunk. Those kids don't know when the men got that money and were gone. There is no need to punish them or the air. They're not the guilty ones." Well, I tell you we could have used mama for the insurance money. She was sorry as sorry could be all over the place. First we didn't know how to calm her raging arms; then we didn't have the power to release her prayerful sorrow. Still we knew that with time she would regain her innocent and unlimited supply of forgiveness and love.

ARCHITECTURE

For: Raymond Fitz

In the brilliant neighborhood of the imagination
Someone always wants to commission a feeling,
To have you set responses on the dotted line.
If you sign the contract, you will discover
You have drawned an obscure mark no one understands
Until some tedious scholar unearths the silence,
Imagines your voice in the dust of signatures
And watches light slowly break around your former words.
It is best to avoid such contractual agreements,
Permit the body to continue with its select functions,
Find its own way through the tender architecture of the body,
The predicament of blood, nerves and bones
Where the skull remains protective of the rigid house of speech.
The heart is the first of four strict rooms.
The hands are second; they dust unfamiliar places.
The eyes reach beyond the windows into the garden
Where the curvaceous figures of Atlas and Venus rest.
They are third in feeling and thrust and pull are fourth.
They are physical revelations;
They set the feet adventurously wandering and the tongue
Wondering about the pure fruit of this structure.
It is finally the scholar who teaches how to tune
The human ear to its own necessities.

A CHILDHOOD MEMORY

I discovered a world among the small stones
In the back alleys of Birmingham, Alabama
Among the papers, bottles and cans which
Were thrown or blown under the houses
Where we used to play hide and seek
With the neighborhood girls who, when
They were caught with their fingers
Uncrossed, or who, maybe, uncrossed them
Intentionally, had to lift their dresses
As punishment until we saw their best secret.
Our inexperienced eyes glazed like frozen water.
In that moment of wonder our fingers relaxed
And the girls trapped us and down came our pants
And up went our embarrassed vanity. Sometimes
The older boys made love with explosive
Sweetness, they said, and that we younger boys
With games still in our eyes, would discover
In time the best game of all beneath our basic skins.

HIS FATHER TAUGHT HIM A FEW LESSONS

Although he never questioned once
the underpinnings of his truths
he spoke about everything,
riding the back of a segregated bus,
drinking colored water,
entering designated toilets
to cast away personal wastes.
He had to learn to devise
a plan to discover
if the architecture
of what he said was true?
By the time he knew the answers,
his father was dead.

A DIFFERENT KIND OF CONVERSATION

For: Henry Louis Gates, Jr.

I am in a purple olive grove
Scratching against the earth of escape.
I am looking for a sweet space
Where I may sow new spare seeds
Where I may breathe sun,
Eat the air, scratch water,
Cause abrasions with my teeth,
Smell a country I have never walked, freely, in.
I am an exile from slavery.
There is only darkness in my bones,
A holiness that is constantly running away.
Hounds are in cold pursuit.
If they trap me
They will feast on the muscles of my breast;
Through that opening in the flesh
They will view the heart of my testicles pulsing
Holding on to the electric road of escape,
That galvanizes my morning travel,
That is hot on my footsteps fleeing
The hook of anger which always sought
To reel me, unsuspectingly, across
The middle passage into cells
And chains of multiple poisons
Which never intended to love me.

ENTERTAINING MEMORY

For: Judy Detrich

The wind sings like ancient birds
Far away in some delicate land.
My words are ancient ancestors
Reigning in a place where
Leaves lay in white pieces on the ground;
Where terror bleeds light
Like a new country moon.
I scar my voice in wax
And watch the excess
Curl and fall to the floor.
I think the sound on that disc
Will entertain your memory of me
In that foreign place, will fall
Like a pure grace upon you
And keep you safe.

SLIGHT OF HAND

The one thing Houdini could never do
Was escape himself
That was a bitter paradox
The window exits of flesh
The eyes never opened easily
Out into the sincere blue
Which infects this planet's sky
Like gum that slides heavily
From those Amazonian trees
Bordering house and heart
White and thick as the mucus of birth
Like strained marshmallows all slowly
Turning blue like dyed eggs
Waiting for justice to pass
Some final sentence
Which will justify peace on
the crack baby desiring to
Enter the world properly.

BREATH

When The Dalai Lama dies
the monks
immediately begin
their arduous search
of locating his
breath descendent,

the child
who was born
at the precise second
the revered man
ceased to breathe;

        it is always the hope

that they have found
the divine alive
and still breathing

so that there never
occurs an interim
in his reign.

APPROPRIATE WORDS FOR MOURNING

for Pablo Neruda

The rain begs at the pailings of the wagon.
The wagon sheds the rain.
The wheels carve deeper roads
Through the rocks and mud
Which are soon flush with water.
The neighbors come out of their houses
One by one carrying grief as a flower.
Pain's what they know.
It is a familiar friend,
Silence is an imposition of law.
Still it can not shackle eye or ear,
For the town knows what it needs to know,
And will say what it must
Through the fiction of their blood,
And the breath of poems.
Neither man nor woman passes away
Without someone knowing,
And that is why these citizens
Have assembled and follow
The faithful rain into the local cemetery
Where all the solemn umbrellas weep
As they place this man
In the earth.

FRAGMENT FOR EMILY DICKINSON

For Chris and Joseph Watras

On that bright Friday morning the
Light flaked through the trees when
I presented my self to your house.
The shades on the second floor were
Drowsy, not quite awake.
The house could not be aroused.
Only the lone meticulous gardener
Could be seen outside trimming
The bushes and lawn. The landmark
Was always closed to strangers.
"You are allowed a curtained presentment,"
The gardener said and continued his
Secular pruning in the fierce presence
Of that sepulchral white house.

IN MEMORY OF CARROLL ARNETT (GOGISGI)

For: Claudia

This Monday morning
The sky is clear:
no clouds,
the grasses are still,
no leaf shudders,
only perilous sun.
This is a good day
to rest.
I listen for wind,
for information
to receive the words
read in your honor
to tune my voice
to their voices
to their rhythms
their specific dance.
I watch the sky
this severe morning
for that special
eagle, whose shadow,
reportedly on that
last day, your burial,
I am told fluttered
a benediction on all
that was taking place.

"SHALOM, CHAVER"

In Memoriam, Yitzhak Rabin, 1922–95

Someone has come and shaken the fruit tree;
birds nesting there were frightened;
all have fluttered away.
Nothing resides in the tree;
an emptiness of snow touches the branches.
Clear frozen ice adheres to these branches.
This winter is without leaves.
The roots of the tree have fallen asleep.
The ground holds steady against the cold.

III. Angel Fury

BLACK VILLANELLE

There was a time when the black men ate first
because the field work demanded a full stomach.
We children always held our laughter and silence,

under the strict moratorium of our mother's eye
lest we unwittingly disturbed our father's sleep.
That was the time when the old men ate first

while our secondary stomachs whined and complained,
the justice of the scraps were left for us to consume,
like children who always held their laughter and silence

because the times required it. We needed to be quiet.
Whatever was necessary the young men brought it home,
for that was the time when the working men ate first.

As persuasive as ever, our joyous voices made noise
outside of the house, in the yards and streets, careful
as children who always held their laughter and silence;

our voices could raise the roof of a black sky,
(and not betray a child who had never understood
that this was a time when the black men ate first)
like children who always held their laughter and silence.

WALKER EVANS' *ALABAMA COTTON TENANT FARMER'S WIFE 1936*

For: Mark and Mariann Callahan

She has made what she could out of this life.
It is spare,
She bites her lips,
Perhaps, tastes her own blood
And knows she will endure.
It looks as if the wind has worn away her beauty
As it has torn away the paint from their clap-board dwelling.
It is the desolate thirties.
The land has long since turned from yielding cotton.
She has Modigliani eyes
They cut through,
They look forward
The time is spent for this brief picture taking.
She will make what she can for dinner
And hold on to what love she has in Alabama.

WALKER EVANS' "ALABAMA TENANT FARMER 1936"

There was once hope in my eyes,
As fresh as my newborn's cries.
She is my survivor; she will break free
From the thinness of dimes,
From the dirt which has insinuated its way
Past skin, blood and bone to some deeper place
Where even the soul has not thought to go.
My daughter is my last gamble;
She will free me from these hills.
She is my way out. I have turned the land
For the very last time. I can do no more,
Nor hope that this marketable year will turn more
Plentiful profit. In the late night, when the house
Breathes in silence, I taste my wife's subtle
Passion; while she can still taste the sun
In my pores. A stone is in me which is blind
To that which I once called hope.

THE GARDEN OF EARTHLY DELIGHT

For: Robert Hayden

Hieronymus Bosch fell into an admirable sleep.
He dreamed: of creamy women with dark adorning
Cherries in their mouths; of a man naturally
Flying under the flatulent power of his body,
Or an old woman perilously balancing a cherry
On the last three stiff hairs of her head.
In the third panel of his dream a platypus
Serves a starving man weeds and bark torn
From the trees of war. An ebony woman wears
A crown of peacocks; the melody in her face
Is terror. The cherry's secret is sealed.
Its skin does not indicate what the polished
Woman knows. She understands why a flying
Fish can be seduced by a fisherman's hook
Sporting a cherry. The taste of mermaid here
Is a dark delirious wine. A syphilitic blonde
Drinks some of this seductive juice. The red
Warms her blood and delights her vision.
Her straw hair teases her shoulders; her moist
Tongue rubs the rim of her glass into sound
Like those which haunts the dreams of Hieronymus
Bosch and where hunger ravishes forbidden fruit.

THE PRIEST

For: Julia, and her 1989 Class
of Communicants

Before he can kiss the nape of his collar
They want to know if he has the power to
Transform the smallest segments of their
Lives like a cook who changes flour and
Water into the thinnest, gentle dough
Which with added heat and perfect air
Will rise to proper flakiness and crust
Over in a uniformly consistent brown?
Who is this vicar whose fleshly hands
Becomes the mystical bread and wine?

DRIVING ACROSS I-70

The highway is littered
with deer carcasses first
struck dumb by automotive
headlights, then by the
sudden acceleration of
it heart facing death.
One such body has lain
so long the ground has
begun to absorb its body
from underneath. Its fur
has become white as dead
grass; its entrails
blackened like stripped
mined cavities gazes
at the rotting sun.
The deer's head is a
vanished trophy. Black
clouds slither across
the rugged terrain,
over the naked remains.
They stop as if to feed
upon necessary food
and then move on
followed by air again.

NEVADA

is the state
where you learn
to be an effective
gambler. I know, with
my favorite friend
dying, I am never
going to be a
successful gambler.
I simply do not know
how to assemble my
assets or toss the dice;
count the faces on cards,
watch the water wheel turn,
the ball, black or white,
spins toward some existential
grey or darker space.
Gamblers, however, need to know
what the explicit chances are,
and what the odds will render?

CURSE

One harvest of black-eyed peas crushed to dust
One football field pig bladder
One venomous Edenic snake
One angel of fury sent to The Garden
One sword of lightening 5000 F
Two agues: pain, and torment
Two sharp garden rake teeth
Forty days of rain
Forty nights of rain

Mix black-eyed pea dust in pig bladder
Add Edenic venom
Slowly add angel fury
Until there is a dust storm
Add one ague at a time
It does not matter which
Add forty days of rain
Add second ague
Gradually begin to stimulate
Mixture with lightening
Stir with giant cement mixer
Until all the ingredients
Have been well mixed
Lay mixture on a large football field

Stimulate continuously
Until mixture reaches 5000 F
Or until bladder reaches
The breaking point
Or when it is as tight as a basketball
Or has the agility of volleyball
Add forty nights of rain
Let cool and age for eighteen year
Release it on its own

NIGHT

The night is a harsh encroachment;
It afflicts the eyes whose lids
Like iron muscles abruptly are
Forced to close to extinguish
That abrasive light which moves
With the speed of sudden pain.
It is a dark which seeps blindly
Under the door jambs and glides
Effortlessly through the panes
Of transoms into the clear visions
Of our lives. There are no noticeable
Pastels to notice like imperceptible
Gestures of love and sorrow observed
From a safe distance. Sometimes
Light is so violent against the
Dark, it can only be contained
Within deceptively tightening pupils.
It is then that the eye shuts down
That sense begins to mount fences
Against any illumination
Approaching those dark holes
We call sight.

NEIGHBOR

Spring is in you
Gentle old Jew
You knew isolated hungers
Like no other communal stomach.
Gentle Sir, you gathered
Dispensable chicken parts,
Carefully cooked and seasoned them,
Then fed the tribe of cats at your back door.
Gentle man, your house is empty now.
The cats, themselves, are
Dispersed like the wind searching
For the unimaginable corners
Of your generous hands.

HUSTLING

This small black boy
learns early how
to sell strangers
goods they do not want.
It is the unwrinkled
nature of his face
which charms. That
will always be
his lucky card.
He holds his
persistent box of
candies: fresh
and stale.
He inquires
about interest
then moves on.
After eight tries
he make a sale.
Everything, he
understands, is
a matter of time.
He is quick
to recognize
that rare light
in the eyes of his
potential customers.
That ray signals
the exact moment
he will make
a profit.

[Philadelphia 05.23.99
London 06.03.99
Dayton 03.22.2002]

CSONTVARY TIVARDAR'S "OLD WOMAN PEELING AN APPLE"

For: Toth Edit

I have heard that the apple is woman failure.
I do not know who first wrongly deposited
That statement in the air, perhaps it came
From the tongues of snakes and men because
They were enthralled by the dark curiosity
In women's eyes. It is a light like no other.
I, on the other hand, have peeled apples,
A careful chore, since I was seven.
I have fed some astounding hungers with them;
I have pared their skins thinly and boiled them
For jellies, sliced the meat from the core
To make turnovers, pies, and sweet sauces.
I have dried the new seeds, planted them,
But never with much success. Nothing new
Has ever come from it. Now my skin darkens
Like peeled apples. I am eighty years into
This process; I use my skills to stay alive.
My husband was never as careful as I learned to be.
He never paused to consider what portions I afforded,
Or what he carelessly left on his plate.
He ate on the run; he died on the run.
That day the house was filled with the aroma of herbs.
I, on the other hand, have never followed his mark.
I never make haste; I am deliberate.
I shall die with this attitude.
So you my grandson must never acknowledge
What I tell you with shame. You will want,
I hope, to be a different man, to move through
Your home, tasting, seeing, breathing and feeling
The passionate textures of those around you,
The flavors of all the things you have gathered.

IV. A Spare Turnip in this Land

THE FIRST EVENING

I watch the flames curl themselves around the logs in the
Fireplace, they suck the timbers of their final juices.
I taste the smell of burning sugar.
I slowly watch the flames continue
To slither like boa constrictor seeking heat
Squeezing the juices from their prey.
They tighten their fatal grip down
To the marrow of the victim's bone.
The logs lay banked for many summer days
Waiting for the first flames of fall to burn and eat them
To ash and warm the chill that lies somewhere
Deep in the carousing room.
As these logs begin to burn
I feel comfort again
I reach into the air
As it warmly passes by.
A seductive shape and form emerges
Eating away at bark, wood and layers of coal.
The smoke weaves a visible blanket of heat at
The hearth's mouth where this idiomatic
Fire with is soft and broken flames all shale.
It is oxygen burning.

THERE ONCE WAS AN OLD WOMAN

who expertly sharpened her kitchen knives
until blue sparks flew like stars before her head.
She said: "I will slice the invasive sunlight
that dares to tread with the footfall of a dinosaur
through my dining room window or upon the transparent
cheesecloth of my kitchen table. I will serve that light
upon a blue plate of pansies with extra culinary dreams.
I will persuade the water meter man who comes to my back door
with seductive whispers, so original, that he will be
unable to resist joining me in a casserole of hay."
There is a quiet determination stored in that house
in the suburb of her heart; a natural blue falls
like a careless negligee around her feet.

DARK PRONOUNCEMENT

Old Miss Molten was preacherly black. She could curse her students
with her left eye, while her right eye proceeded with the business
of roll calling. You knew, at once, you would never recover from
the curse of that left eye or stem the tide of its powers. This was
more than suggested fear. It all came true especially if she took a
          mind to
voice a specific opinion about your future. Her tongue was full of
          terrible
assurances. So when my time came, and it did, she
warned me fully that: "You will never succeed without Maurice; he is
your worldly insurance against failure."

So, here I am years later trying to function alone, fighting an average
existence, not knowing which direction Maurice took for his life,
          because
in our youth, we lost touch with each other, and as we moved our
          separate
ways, I realized that moving eradicates as imperceptively as a sudden
          snow
fall. Soon you forget that promise to write, or discover you have no
forwarding address to send your regulated thoughts to. The rest
          becomes a
memory that takes up formal residence behind the eyes.

My mother who was equally never at a loss for astonishing meta-
          phor said
to me with the same dark clarity of a curse: "You will, for all intents
and purposes, end up shitting and stepping in it. You will need an
          expert
recipe for cleaning the scent from your shoes."

It is amazing to me now, how those two voices merged layer upon
          layer like
the skin of my life. I step with caution, and try to avoid the thick
          tongue
of truth. I glide my feet along true and necessary longitudes: the
perimeters of stone, wood, and old macadams. I realize it is not mere

luck
or chance that Maurice and I do not touch paths any longer. Our
      boyhoods
cannot be assessed by a reasoned brain. What does the brain
      know of curses?
I try to stand clear of the grey prophesies of old women, and
      practice
friendship within the close proximity of what the human hands
      can accomplish.

ELVIS PRESLEY'S FIRST APPEARANCE ON THE ED SULLIVAN SHOW

Miss Rosie Mae,
sitting in the living room
watching The Ed. Sullivan Show
sucked in her pious lips
smacked them clean as any sectarians,
watching from Los Angeles to the Adirondacks,
and uttered with her skeptical voice
of motherly concentration:
"Those little girls are too fast for words."
Every time his thigh would quiver
as if he were writing
down some invisible numbers
or vast phrases to thrill the blood,
those tv girls would scream
a lightening jolt again and again.
Then Miss Rosie Mae would point to the screen
as if a million girls had, all of a sudden,
given up the privacy of their bodies wholly
especially when Sullivan announced:
"For the first time on our stage,
here to perform for you this evening,
is the new singing sensation Elvis Presley."
The cheers never allowed us to hear again.
I never knew a guitar had so many seductive moves;
I never knew a guitar could win so many innocent lips.
They testified loudly when his guitar twitched;
They shivered, as if touched by the Holy Ghost
when the chords tickled the loneliness
in their thighs.
"It is dangerous to watch that young man
from the waist down. He's pure sex,"
Miss Rosie Mae said.
"Somebody, somewhere needs to give those
little girls a pinch of saltpeter,
maybe a little more than a pinch if you ask me.
Elvis uttered his songs on a ledger of air;

he sang with such a vengeance
that every young girl felt
as if he was singing only to her,
that she had received her proper potion
and could cheer, unreservedly,
her blood into infinite hoarseness.

HURRYING

From his house to hers was exactly 150 miles door to door.
After her stroke and subsequent amputation
Duty drove him up the highway.
When he arrived, he began his immaculate chores immediately.
The first was washing, combing and plaiting his mother's hair.
He imitated what he had seen her do for his stray sisters.
He and his mother began this chore
At the plentifully large kitchen sink.
He hurried; she could stand for an hour
On the one leg she had left.
The process could not last too long;
They would argue.
He was the adult; she had become the child.
He always hoped as he stroked the brush through her hair
He had pulled it another luxurious inch longer.
His fingers rushed to keep pace with his mother's endurance.
"First, make sure the water floods the scalp," she said.
"Second, shampoo every area of scalp rapidly; don't waste time.
Tickle the skull with riotous fingers.
Use your fingernails to dig in if you must.
Third, when you come to rinse my head, do as the Baptist do.
Severely dunk my hair! Be careful to remove all the suds.
Some are bound to try and hide like subversive sins.
They must be cleansed like sinners seeking redemption.
Four, five and six," she ordered,
"Dry, oil, then plait like you were dancing for the devil.
Set the plaits in strict corn rows," was the last of her commands.
His fingers raced up and down the natural curves of her skull.
Hurrying caused his fingers to veer from the narrow confines
Of her scalp; oftentimes the plaits were crooked,
But the hair was clean and freshly oiled.
His hands were never able to manufacture French braids
Only negotiate those awkward male plaits
Which had never been tutored or trained to join one another.
Out of hurried necessity,
Haste was the clean invitation to trouble.
That is when his appendages lost all of their accuracy.

Time was the inevitable thorn which stabbed their nerves,
So that, at the end of this one chore,
They were glad that the task was accomplished
With as little loss of blood as possible:
The mother for her hour of patiently standing on her one leg,
The son, for hurrying.

THE SEASON OF WAR

I have lost recognition of the true sense of time
There are moments when I do not know what day it is
Right now I do not know what week it is
And if I am truthful, I do not know what month
Or worse yet what year it is that we are occupying
I have lost all sense of seasons
I do not know when the Spring ended
Nor when the Summer began;
I recognize only two seasons:
The season of war; the season of peace
I do not know when the latter will Fall
But I can tell you that the empty Winter came first
And now there is only a steady falling snow

WHERE THE WILD NETTLES GROW

My black African brothers
Take aim at me kneeling
Prayerfully for my patriotic
Revolt. Despair enters the
Skull of my spirit. Oh, my
Countrymen do not smile
At the damage your bullets
Will do as they glide
Through the grey of my brain.
Blood and brains stir our
Resolve to newer solutions.
This land is mother and
Father to us both, and
Though it hold my naked body
First, it is prepared
To hold yours as well.
Only decency covers my groin.
Dignity is a spare turnip
In this land. It is the blood
Of angers nourishes them
In that plot of land
Where wild nettles grow.

V. Blue Unannounced Satellites

HERE

For: James and Linda Chervenka

Beyond the point where the exquisite marble left off,
The wooden stairs in this old theatre have become
So narrow that only one body may pass.
High above everything, only birds can speak.
The air here is thin as frayed threads.
A friend wants to introduce me to
The silk presence she has felt.
She has watched the dust flicker on these benches.
I listen for the same sacred rattle,
For echoes of laughter gone stale,
Of applause so old the bones crack.
Light is muted here,
Ancient horrors in the steeled dust.
It patches the worn floors
Where rejection hangs like old humidity
Unable to evaporate. Here old neglect
Lies covered under a thin membrane of dust
Waiting for the clean chance to again infect.

SLEEPING LOVERS

For: Phillip John Shaw

There they were positioned in the waiting room of the local
bus station, asleep in each other's arms, when suddenly,
without warning, they were instant gasoline and flames.
Fire itched into their flesh like the tight curls on
his dark neck, and the long straight ones which dangled
like gold from her fair head. It was the abidingly cool
smell of the gasoline and the joyful fire's tickle that
caused these two to dance wildly like Holiness Witnesses
fingered by the Holy Ghost, like puppets in a conflagration
until they fell, smothering each other on the ground in
a heap of flesh, hair, blood and bare bones, becoming
collectors' items, someone's common vision, a naked
brutality, the general hostility of a father's father's
father's teachings. These lovers did not exit this life
singing into a peacefully cinematic dawn. They had one
utterable and civilized love. It was tested with flames
by these certain youths who made, in that terminal, a dark
monument to Siegfried and Brunhilde while listening to the
song of secrecy propagated by a father's father's father's
father's laughter.

PAINFUL LAUGHTER

It must have been this way when Roland Hayes first sang in Germany. What, the *literati* thought, can this small black man do with our sacred lieder? Then he floated, effortlessly, the enchanting melodies of Schubert's *Du bist die ruh* from his dark lips, an unexpected torrential downpour of Ruckert's cool summer words flooded the walls and they began to reverberate. Surprise was forever etched on the tongues of those in the audience who began to cheer and cheer and cheer this brown man who came from the southern clay and cotton of Curryville, Georgia. What did they know? What did they know about the birth of song or in what soil it could take root.

ADVERTISEMENT

Husband Wanted:

None but those with the following refined qualities need apply; *you must possess the ability to tickle silk; you need not possess the static cling of electricity; you must be willing to love any woman named julie ann pizza and enter her life with hat in hand preferably riding a palomino of distinguished breed vowing to be a party to everything the horse is inclined to do; you must hate zits and do everything possible to erradicate them from the body politic; you must love bubble gum and children on hot blue days as well as those days which are exactly opposite because I am a woman who requires it. I do not wish to present myself as niggling on the subject; I want to be clear and non-deceptive, otherwise there would be no wisdom whatsoever in my having paid for this advertisement.*

LIGHT ANOINTS

The light anoints strange dreams. Silence whips our tongues. Gunpowder is despair poured like pickling brine over our faulty wounds. I instruct my bearded captor to desist. I eat the earth willfully. I am quick silver, I say *let all die who were miserably born, let their spirits feed sharks. Waste no human blood otherwise.* Dust is in the air, it binds, it strangles, it offers no compromise. *O my dead sisters, O my dead brothers, O my dead ancestors, death is a chore which struggles with rhythm, with the pulse of the drums, with the songs of the inner ear.* History does not suffer; the truth has been spat in the wind.

WEDDING POEM

For: Ronan and Elizabeth

My one single desire above all others is the gift given to mankind, the pleasure of meditation, to be able to question at once the all astonishing rainbow and ask why, even with the world surrounding us with a whimsical silence relishing that the world would only answer with hysterical laughter. I will not practice forgetfulness nor remember every birthday you have experienced, in the pastures of love, so that you will not feel betrayed by the fire in my skeleton, realizing all the while that love, like nature, is blind and that its icily conviction is maintained by the anticipatory conviction that the heart will always be in an imperative state of *behold my heart*, without modern cholesterol, *is ready to commend my body to fire or sword,* so that you might suffer worldly peace. *Let all my bones cry out against dogs, trees, weapons, fires, the ordinary torments of hell, great or small as they might be, demonstrating the work of physicians, with the magical distinction of a necromancer, who beyond the imagined thoughts of ordinary time, reason or joy, affords me the public opportunity to testify with human breath, marrowed imagination and hearty blood that I do sacredly love you woman.*

HUNTED AGAIN

In Memory: Jay Hoffman

My father's death came like a hard roll of the dice rattling against
a wire cage, tossed across a felt embankment, and finally stopping
at some grave unanticipated number. It was just such a noise that
rattled in his lungs, ice cubes chinking in crystal waiting to break
under the thin stream of liquor in a place where warm music is
often found. He died of a casual cigarette, white, burning to
exquisite ash, an ecstasy he would not forgo until it finally killed
him, left him and his still body wrapped in that dark aroma he
couldn't let go of.
I, in my perfect young witness, kept him from that wry embrace
he would have willingly entered. He told me of the exotic
seductive warmth that every man, like himself, wished for,
searched for and hungered to taste. He knew he would never
escape. I hung on to the good in him as long as I could and then I
let go. His dying was not easy to watch; one late afternoon
between a hard martini and the aroma of strong morning coffee,
he surrendered. He had insisted on dying with his eyes open so
nothing would ever surprise him again.

THE BROKEN VESSEL

In memory of Leonard Port

I think of you friend, from time to time, as memory makes necessary. I know Buffalo, beneath its blankets of snow was never kind to us; there was too much cold in the air, too much distance, and the sun never came as it should have. The people around us, who were our friends never learned our names. It was that same white cold, that cancerous silica, infecting itself softer than dust moving like crazed atoms in sunlight. Such a white killed your wife and murdered your spirit too. Knowledge, in those days, was a dangerous pursuit; still we sought it in every crack and crevice because it tasted like Greek grapes to our tongues; the juices ran like beautiful rivers flooding heart and brain. We were drunk with knowing. At what known hour did I lose your generous speech? Once you came to my door, you brought me assurance when I did not, especially, believe in song any longer. What a music it was that you made with the silence in my head, bright and active as the chaos of maggots attacking rot in spring trees filled with the bright leaves of sun and the green water of leaves. So it was that you came, unexpectedly, that morning knocking with an insistent soft touch; so it was that affecting hand was soon gone when I was far away from its ability to love. Buffalo, I say, was never loving to you or me; I do not forget. I know it loved some of us better than it did others; cities are like that.

BACKGROUND

A young black southerner looks into the eyes of another
southerner. He sees two rings of blue, unannounced satellites; he
wonders aloud: "Is your license true when it says your eyes are
brown?" The one southerner tells his counterpart no one knows
the origin of the blue in his ancestry. There are always plenty of
rumors to spread like sticky jam especially when the mothers and
fathers are both dead, and both sets of grandparents are long
dead. Someone can always suppose but never know. How can
anyone speak truthfully of southern history or what they might
have thought was truthful? When all the descendants of contrib-
uting genes are buried in various unknown cemeteries no one
shall ever know where the blue in my eyes came from; we can
surmise that there was a white woman of European extraction
somewhere lurking in the coal bins of one of my ancestor's
background, but we shall never know for certain; we simply shall
never know.

SUMMER TOURIST

When Rudolph Serkin came to play the pianoforte in Queen Elizabeth Hall I wore a new cheesecloth coat I purchased in Stockholm. The coat wheezed and whined through the first movement of a Beethoven sonata; a patron shushed the coat; she had not come to hear it, nor to have Beethoven relegated to modern music; she had come to savor nuance and subtly, and so I held my muscles in perfect stillness, strained to keep my skin immovable, even, while my blood raced at a steady pace through my veins. I could not stop neither blood nor breath; I was mannequin for the remaining *andante*. Why had Beethoven had such an innovative period; why was he so bent on breaking form and tradition? Who was he my nerves cried? A pause came before the next movement and a gentle hand reached forward and held the nape of my coat while I slid forward out of that coat which held me, painless prisoner, for nearly thirty minutes. A sudden "Thank You" exploded from my body like a hidden mind listening for the perfect note.

BLACK PROMETHEUS

Nothing beyond the ancestry of African American whose bodies were thrown up against the walls of southern cities where the leashed hounds snarled, snapped and ate the daily livers. They were, in fact, the fresh flesh which stood against the guards who turned their hoses on the fires of discontent. What they had done with their patient blood heritage, their dark fore-fathers could not have anticipated nor dared. These were a new generation of souls who found renewal, the knowledge of what their fathers longed for: a piece of sunlight, the smell of rest in the evening winds. They took energy from the silver abuse of fire, a curse of words, from sunshine born to excite the heart from those people retired and living their quiet lives as far away as good Ohio. This was the time of dissipation, of holy testament, holy and black as *The Bible*. "Death was nothing to them," sang the children in memory of those who found themselves bound to the rocks of the surrounding city. Their places are secure on higher shoulders with courteous blood so that new sons and new daughters might greet each other with diplomacy and a saner "hello" than ever greeted their parents.

GRAPES

ripe and filled to the sensuous skin of harvesting.
the sanskrit tree holds within its grasp the fruit of faith
no dog would dare bark armageddon at or make cacophonous
        noises
like the pernicious giraffe of a child who was never candid
about reaching for unattainable fruits of friendships.
humidity of fragrance hangs like steel no athlete could lift,
and when his simple hand moved upwards towards its flesh,
the fruit pulled back with striking ease.
the air seemed to suspend it no matter how loudly the fans
        cheered.
nothing could bring that harvest down within reach of desiring
fingers. we were instructed to be patient, that the richness of
the tree, continually brimming, bears only bitterness to the
tongue. what lies we ate in those days when lightening electrified
the air; when it burned the synapses and we took axe to the tree.
We found new implements of justice to change the roots of growing.

AMERICAN GOTHIC

There is no southern record of my mother or father standing next to each other with uncommon grace like these two stand. If they were next to each other it was with the pitch forks aimed solidly at each other's heart. If fate contrived to have them stand next to each other it was out of the predestined fear that they could do nothing to alter their position or condition. They were there, as we are all here, inextricably bound by our different natures to the spaces we must occupy. There is no northern record that they slept comfortably next to each other. There were never any muffled sounds in my nightmares. What were their lives like: work, eating for renewed strength, sleep and then work again? So what would they think of me now making poems out of their indifference without the slightest recognition for space, time, community, love or personal house to thresh out their spare lives in?

ESCAPE TO THE PROMISED LAND

My hypodermic pencil records, with truth, how my father, one day, came home drunk as a blind man and pissed up and down the street publicly. Auntie and Mother's Dear's Christian sensibility was mortified that day, fried in the summer sun like an egg fallen to the sidewalk from its nest. Mother Dear told Mama, "Get somewhere for you and your child to go." They never mentioned whether we had to take my father or no. So with careful ignorance they split that marriage asunder. Mama said "I never protested or questioned what had to be done. I marshalled my brains and found somewhere for you and me to go. We made do on faith and prayer. After a dark room in someone else's house, we came to public housing. For years jugging every new penny I got as a raise we managed to keep the rent in check, and saved enough on the side that God saw fit to deliver us into our first modest home where we painted and cleaned, and made a firm foundation among the Baptists, Methodists and Lutherans in the neighborhood. We took in several roomers, but only the men survived the extraordinary demands on cleanliness that I made. I hated a filthy house. What woman is worth her salt living in such filth? I even went so far as to teach you how to cook and clean. I couldn't be there every hour; I had to work to get food and keep the bill collectors at a distance."

I remember all those poor women; no one could have been that imperfect. All the Eves of my life driven from us with sharp and haughty words! Our home was paradise; it was the heavenly kingdom where we worked. No maid ever worked out when Mama was in charge. No one could ever vault over her standard, and if by chance they reached it accidently, they could not maintain the intensity and fell by the wayside like so much chaff. Like all the Eves before me, I decided to walk into freedom. Self-containment. She had trained me well; I had a Depression will to survive. No jumping out of windows for me. I was nourished on the tenacious notion that something better was coming and that is how, one day in a bright August sun, I crossed the George Washington Bridge into New York City and never looked back.

VIRUS

The stomach suddenly rebels
contracts into pure arches
releases an inadvertent
gun-burst of food digested,
undigested and rancid
green to the naked eye.
The mouth is a volcano;
it splays an inconceivable
canvas on the local ground.
A wild, an unknown virus
knocks starch from the bones,
leaves the left pectorals
stiff, in an exhaustion of pain,
like Alvin Ailey's lithe dancers
challenging the intricacies
of air space light and time.
Muscles transports
inexorable stations of delight.

TO BEDLAM AND BACK

place of chaos

Take the man without any shoes to bedlam
Take the woman who is ironing her dues to bedlam
Take the child who has never spoken any words to bedlam
Take all my distant relatives over the mountain
and those who are securely dead,
placed in the cemetery and the rest who are named
Woodward in my grandfather's will, take them to bedlam.
All the people rising from nightly sleep to brush each other's
teeth with pastel toothpaste, send them instantly to bedlam.
Take all those who adhere to no cannon to bedlam.
Take all those men who have abandoned vanity to bedlam
as well as the ladies who espouse peace instead of ethnic love
to bedlam, to bedlam, to bedlam with them all.
Let all those who are paying attention,
as a public announcement, hear this final pronouncement
as a commendation to go to bedlam.
Let all those who occupied Hungary
as a necessary program,
and all those missing whose happiness
was appropriated reside in bedlam.
May their lives be as exciting
as a truck that metamorphoses
into pure Spring quizzical blue,
paranoid as an eight day old
tight armpit of a crocodile
that practices exacerbation
and wickedness as all evil doers
who, having done the deed,
must be put into the cells of bedlam
by Batman or his likely component
who, wanting to save us all,
in an ultimate act of compassion,
must do good.
When hate becomes a full fledged citizen
take me to bedlam
When men and women no longer argue about love
take me to bedlam

When there is no longer a love of laughter
take me to bedlam
When all the wizards of money have lost their greed
take me to bedlam
When all the songs of love have vanished like wisps of smoke
take me to bedlam
When there is no more music in the land
I require you send me to bedlam
When there are no more weavers of trees
take me to bedlam
When there are no more priests of the dark
take me to bedlam
When there are no more governmental liars
take me rejoicing into bedlam
When the horizon shrinks to a twenty-eight waistline
take me successfully to bedlam
When there are no more countries laid to waste and muck
take me to bedlam
When there are no more threaders of the air
take me to bedlam
When there are no more seamstresses of water
take me to bedlam
When there are no more engineers of plastic
take me to bedlam
When there is no longer a tailor of twigs
take me to bedlam
When there is no longer a master builder of infinitesimal clouds
take me to bedlam
When we can not locate a single carpenter of cement
take me to bedlam
When there are no longer shoemakers of steel
take me to bedlam
When the last manicurist of grass no longer works
take me to bedlam
When there are no more magicians who understand fog
take me to bedlam
When the last orgasm is preserved in clear plastic
take me to bedlam
When the last beautician has to contend with unthinkable trash
take me to bedlam

When the last racist turns into beneficent moonlight
I will gladly welcome bedlam
When the last visionary is blind
I shall gladly go to bedlam
When all the land is evenly patched
I shall gladly knock at the door of bedlam
When all the rough roads in the plain sky are smooth
bedlam will be here
When all the rough color has faded from the sky
take me to bedlam
When all the names on all the headstones are erased
take me to bedlam
When all the bones and their dust are resurrected
take me to bedlam
When the last McDonalds has been sold and counted
take me to bedlam
When the last exit and the last way out has been shut
I will be in bedlam
When all the coca cola has been drunk
take me to bedlam
When all the lawyers have pleaded their own guilt
O, take me to bedlam
When the last tobacco reed has been extinguished
take me to bedlam
When Caballe has had the final opportunity to sing
I shall have arrived at the gate of bedlam

———————— ❦

Herbert Woodward Martin is presently Poet-In Residence at The University of Dayton where he teaches creative writing and African American Literature. He is the author of six volumes of poetry. His sixth volume won The Edwin Mellen First Prize for poetry. This is his seventh volume to be published.

Herbert Woodward Martin has been associated with the Dayton Poet Paul Laurence Dunbar for more than a quarter century. During that association he has written and produced *Paul Laurence Dunbar: The Eyes of the Poet*, and he has edited *In His Own Voice: The Dramatic and Other Uncollected Works of Paul Laurence Dunbar*. He was the librettist for Adolphus Hailstork's opera *Paul Laurence Dunbar: Common Ground*. Martin has served as librettist for Philip Magnuson's opera *It Pays To Advertise* as well as his *Magnificat*. He recently wrote a libretto for Adolphus Hailstork's cantata *Crispus Attucks*.

Herbert Woodward Martin is the recipient of The Ohio Governor's Award, The Ohioana Award for Drama and an Ohio Arts Council Fellowship and two Montgomery County Arts and Cultural District Fellowships. From 1990 to 1991 he was a Fulbright Scholar to The University of Pecs in Pecs, Hungary.

Bottom Dog Press
****** Working Lives Series ******
http://members.aol.com/lsmithdog/bottomdog

Robert Flanagan. *Loving Power: Stories*. 1990/ 0-933087-17-9 $8.95
A Red Shadow of Steel MIlls: Photos and Poems. 1991
(Includes Timothy Russell, David Adams, Kip Knott, Richard Hague)
0-933087-18-7 $8.95
Chris Llewellyn. *Steam Dummy & Fragments from the Fire: Poems*. 1993/ 0-933087-29-2 $8.95
Larry Smith. *Beyond Rust: Stories*. 1996 / 0-933087-39-X $9.95
Getting By: Stories of Working Lives. 1996
eds. David Shevin and Larry Smith / 0-933087-41-1 $10.95
Human Landscapes: Three Books of Poems. 1997
(Includes Daniel Smith, Edwina Pendarvis, Philip St. Clair)/
0-933087-42-X $10.95
Richard Hague. *Milltown Natural: Essays and Stories from a Life*. 1997
0-933087-44-6 $16.95 (cloth)
Maj Ragain. *Burley One Dark Sucker Fired*. 1998 / 0-933087-45-4 $9.95
Brooding the Heartlands: Poets of the Midwest, ed. M.L.Liebler. 1998
0-933087-50-0 $9.95
Writing Work: Writers on Working-Class Writing. 1999
eds. David Shevin, Larry Smith, Janet Zandy / 0-933087-52-7 $10.95
Jim Ray Daniels. *No Pets: Stories*. 1999/ 0-933087-54-3 $10.95
Jeanne Bryner. *Blind Horse: Poems*. 1999 / 0-933087-57-8 $9.95
Naton Leslie. *Moving to Find Work: Poems*. 2000 / 0-933087-61-6 $9.95
David Kherdian. *The Neighborhood Years*. 2000 / 0-933087-62-4 $9.95
Our Working Lives: Short Stories of People and Work. 2000
eds. Bonnie Jo Campbell and Larry Smith / 0-933087-63-2 $12.95
Allen Frost. *Ohio Trio: Fictions*. 2001/ 0-933087-68-3 $10.95
Maj Ragain. *Twist the Axe: A Horseplayer's Story* 2002/
0-933087-71-X $10.95
Michael Salinger. *Neon: Stories & Poems*. 2002 / 0-933087-72.1 $10.95
David Shevin. *Three Miles from Luckey: Poems*. 2002 /
0-933087-74-8 $10.95
Working Hard for the Money: America's Working Poor in Stories, Poems, and Photos. 2002, eds. Mary E. Weems and Larry Smith /
0-933087-77-2 $12.95
Jeanne Bryner. *Eclipse: Stories*. 2003 / 0-933087-78-0 $12.95
Richard Hague. *Alive in Hard Times: Poems*. 2003 / 0933087-83-7 $12.00
Paola Corso. *Death by Renaissance: Poems & Photos*. 2004 /
0933087-86-1 $12.00
Jeff Vande Zande. *Emergency Stopping & Other Stories*. 2004
0-933087-87-X $12.95

Titles in the Harmony Series
Bottom Dog Press

America Zen: A Gathering of Poets
eds. Ray McNiece and Larry Smith
0-933087-91-8 224 pgs. $15.00

In Neck Deep: Stories from a Fisherman by Jay Zimmerman
0-933087-90-X 256 pgs. $15.00

Hymns and Songs of Purandaradasa
translated by Dinesh Hassan
0-933087-89-6 88 pgs. $12.95

Song That Fathoms Home: Poems by Ray McNiece
0-933087-85-3 124 pgs. $12.00

Bowl of Water: Poems by Allen Frost
0-933087-88-8 136 pgs. $12.95

O Taste and See: Food Poems
edited by David Lee Garrison & Terry Hermsen
0-933087-82-9 198 pgs. $14.00

Songs of the Woodcutter:
Zen Poems of Wang Wei and Taigu Ryokan
by Larry Smith & Monte Page
0-933087-80-2 (CD & Booklet) $15.00

When: Poems by Don Moyer
0-933087-81-0 96 pgs. $10.95

Supporting the Art of Writing
Homepage for Ordering
http://members.aol.com/Lsmithdog/bottomdog
Include $1.50 with any order for shipping.

———————————— ❧

———————————————— ଓଃ